Paul Lynch:

The Lyrical Alchemist -

Unveiling the Life, Global

Impact and Achievements

of a Renowned Irish

Storytelling Master

Daxton Thomas

Copyright page

Table of contents

Introduction

Paul Lynch is a shining star of poetic genius in the world of Irish writing, known for stories that move people to tears.

Writer Paul Lynch is one of the most revered figures in the world, and for good reason: his lyrical prose and deep understanding of the human condition have enchanted readers all across the globe.

Lynch reaches new artistic heights in Prophet Song, his Booker Prize-winning novel, by creating a word symphony that reverberates with profound philosophical insight and emotional profundity.

He has permanently marked the Irish and global literary landscape with his works, solidifying his status as a literary icon.

In Prophet Song, we follow a young man as he searches for his life's purpose against the haunting backdrop of Ireland in the 1960s.

Lynch skillfully depicts a nation navigating transition and development through the interweaving of the protagonist's issues with the larger social and cultural backdrop of the age.

Lynch weaves a beautiful tapestry of descriptive language into his text, which takes the reader on a mesmerizing literary journey. His words twirl and dance, a captivating tune that reflects the intricacies of being human.

Lynch was born and raised in Ireland, where he developed an early and insatiable need for narrative. Red Sky in the Morning, his first book, showcased his distinctive combination of lyricism, psychological complexity, and vivid storytelling.

Lynch has showcased his command of language and talent for capturing the nuances of human feeling in every one of his outstanding novels, which he has published during his lengthy career.

With his critically acclaimed 2016 book Grace, Lynch won the coveted Kerry Group Irish Novel of the Year prize. The magnificent prose and profound examination of universal issues in this moving story of love, sorrow, and redemption further cemented Lynch's status as a literary giant.

Lynch explores universal truths via the protagonist's life-altering experiences, including love's transformational power, loss's painful sting, faith's consoling solace, and doubt's haunting shadows. Lynch, who has a sharp understanding of human nature, shows us the complex web of feelings that determines our lives and pulls us into the protagonist's inner battles and victories.

Prophet Song is an exceptional work of literature, showcasing Paul Lynch's remarkable talent as a storyteller; it goes beyond being a mere novel. His words have a way of resonating in the mind like a tune of profound beauty and wisdom, even after the last page is turned.

This honor cemented Lynch's position as a literary giant, elevating him to the level of Ireland's most lauded authors.

Lynch is highly regarded not only for his literary talent but also for his steadfast devotion to his work, his need for knowledge about the human condition, and his magical wordplay.

His novels go beyond being just stories; they are explorations of the human condition that shed light on the intricacies of love, grief, faith, and the resilience of the human soul.

Get ready to be captivated as you explore the pages of this tribute to Paul Lynch and his literary genius.

Gain a deeper knowledge of the man behind the magnificent words through personal experiences from people who have had the luxury of knowing him, intelligent analysis from literary experts, and extracts from his acclaimed novels.

Discover the enchantment that has propelled Paul Lynch to the ranks of literature's greatest masters as you lose yourself in the characters' complex emotions and the lush prose of his works.

He should allow his words to carry him away as they inspire, astound, and serve as a reminder of how narrative can influence our lives.

Chapter one

Growing Up in Ireland: A Love of Storytelling from an Early Age

Paul Lynch has a reputation for delving deeply into intricate topics through his beautiful prose.

The Irish city of Limerick is the site of Paul Lynch's birth on May 9, 1977. Now he's 46 years old.

Lynch showed an early aptitude for storytelling, being engrossed in books and able to transport himself to other worlds with fantastical characters and fascinating stories.

The literary love that Lynch inherited from his parents, who were both teachers, was crucial in his development as a writer.

His parents uprooted him from his birthplace in County Donegal in northern Ireland's Ulster region when he was nine months old, and he spent his childhood there.

His father's employment with what was formerly the Coast and Cliff Rescue Service—later renamed the Irish Marine Emergency Service and now known as the Irish Coast Guard—prompted his family to relocate to Inishowen.

His father had a career as an English teacher and had introduced him to the works of great writers; his mother had a career as an Irish literature teacher and had given him an appreciation for the strength and beauty of the Irish language.

Paul's family eventually made their home on the northern peninsula of Inishowen in Ulster, where Lynch spent his formative years between Malin Head and Carndonagh.

In 1995, he departed from County Donegal.

There are three children in Paul Lynch's family.

Up there, everything is barren. The wind is still audible to this day. Somewhere in my mind, I can still sense the sky above. That's well-ingrained in my mind. It's fundamental. Beyond that, my writing is fundamental. On his way to school one day, he was walking to the car when he felt the wind knock him off his feet.

A slight concussion was the result of his head banging. And that is the most recent event in my life.

At one in the morning, he contacted his parents to deliver the news.

For them, it was all part of a fantastical story. What a few years it has been for me.

Like Eilish in the book, his mother was an adult literacy instructor; she started him reading at the age of four using flash cards made from cereal boxes.

They couldn't keep me in books, he remembers, explaining that when he was eleven years old, his mother found me working in a used bookshop. In terms of shaping who I am now, she's a huge presence for me.

Chapter two

Literary Beginnings: Examining Lynch's Thematic Depth through an Analysis of Recurring Themes and Motifs

Paul Lynch's background as a film critic explains why his debut book draws equally from cinematic and literary sources.

Red Sky in Morning 2013:

This book is, in theory, historical fiction because it takes place in the early 1800s when both the United States and Ireland were experiencing the brutal march of civilization and ruthless landlords who were eager to expel their tenants.

Historical events that the audience may recognize form the basis of the plot. The imaginative elements and careless disregard for historical accuracy and nuance, however, set it free from this type of classification.

Issues of recollection, remorse, and reparation are probed.

Amid the misery of their impending eviction, Coll Coyle and his family wake up to a blood-red morning in Inishowen. Only in the last pages does the Coyles' mystery about why the young landlord, Hamilton, has impulsively evicted them from their home and fields come to light.

Coll kills Hamilton in a fit of despair and wrath, forcing him to flee.

Faller, the foreman, decides to go after Coll on his own. His intention to accompany him to the moon and back becomes obvious very quickly. No one gets a good explanation for his obsession with getting even with Hamilton, but the pursuit continues nevertheless.

Coll barely avoids Faller as he stutters and writhes his way across the Co. Donegal wilderness.

When he finally gets to Derry, he robs a bank to buy passage to New York. As Faller exacts his vengeance on his associates, chaos and murder ensue behind him.

Although Coll is currently safe, the relentless fight for survival continues. Amid the majestic sky and sea, the ship is a magnificently constructed battleground where you must watch your back and endure the horrors of sickness and death.

Coll believes the flashy claims of a man named Duffy, an entrepreneur who is recruiting Irishmen to cut the new railroad after he arrives in New York. Ashore at

Duffy's Cut, where cholera and brutal assault claimed the lives of many men, Coll and his shipmate, the Cutter, arrive at the site of the notorious real-life disaster.

Coll toils away, hoping against hope that things will improve and against the possibility of illness or disappointment.

But Faller is pursuing him. Here, the plot thickens into a nail-biter. Is he going to find his prey?

There are more narrow escapes where Faller portrays the monster from a horror film, constantly popping up with his mysterious grin.

Once a mysterious figure, he now reduces himself to the mentality of a crazy gunman, turning into that iconic horseman from Westerns who rides gimlet-eyed over ridges and ravines, taking lives in the process.

It also appears as the story jumps around in time. It could be because we're moving from the damp, desolate, and forested Donegal to the rich, red-roofed fields of Pennsylvania, but at this point, the story takes on a tone that seems to be from a different era, maybe even decades later.

The good person, Coll, has more layers. Feelings of love, loss, and loyalty are bestowed upon him.

A ribbon that belonged to his tiny daughter, whom he had to leave behind, is his only remembrance of home. This has another lovely cinematic touch.

But he lacks the distinctiveness necessary to fully materialize as he blends into the prototypical human mass and the mighty natural environments around him.

Despite its thriller elements, this book relies heavily on atmosphere and evocation to captivate readers. Having a passion for language—both for what it can convey and for describing things in a new way—is the author's first and foremost passion.

This is a noble goal, and he accomplishes it with remarkable and commendable regularity. On occasion, he excels at it.

Furthermore, it's a style of writing that prioritizes itself above all else.

The reversal of adjectives and nouns Repetition makes the tiny road seem invasive, as do flashy substitutes; sleeveless coats are worn instead of worn; the sun is shrouded in clouds; and evenings are filled rather than ended.

This style sways too much between an unabashed desire to stand out and an awkward blend of modernism and a Kiltartan picturesque.

However, Lynch's cinematic prose includes more than just color use. Some of the author's favorite techniques include placing an image at the beginning of a phrase and then contrasting it with an action, such as the splash of water slapping onto hard ground, and then he awoke.

As an example of Lynch's participle idiom, consider the following: sullen sky came down to the land, and he walked with the fleece around his neck. A nineteenth-century Irish farmer's sing-song, repeating speaking patterns are reflected in this verb ping-ponging, which creates the illusion of ongoing motion.

This is not a delicate work, despite the beautiful words; it dabbles in incest, torture, and cholera. We lean into a beautiful reverie while simultaneously clutching our stomachs, thanks to the poetic language and the intense tension created by the combination of gut-wrenching or brain-spilling subject matter.

Because of the strong connection between violent acts and acts of kindness, this is even more significant. Coyle remained whispering to it like it was a lover after slitting the animal's neck to make the blackened stew, which aided in the animal's recovery from the wound.

Unfortunately, clarity might sometimes be sacrificed for poetics in this too-attentive language.

Both the Premier Roman and the French Meilleur Livre Étranger prizes were considered for Paul's first novel, Red Sky in the Morning.

The Black Snow 2014:

Red Sky in the Morning, Paul Lynch's debut novel, was lyrically violent and made the Irish countryside seem like a huge, undefined expanse of land rather than a closely connected, rural community.

However, in his 1945 novel The Black Snow, an Irish emigrant returns to his home country, and that seemingly endless distance starts to flow backward.

Issues of displacement, resilience, and violence are all touched upon in the book.

Barnabas Kane has a successful farm in Donegal with his American wife, Escra, and their teenage son, Billy, after working for several years in New York's construction industry.

However, tragedy comes at the very opening of the story when a barn full of cattle and a farmhand are destroyed in a fire, setting the stage for a gripping tale of mounting suspense.

After escaping the void that swallowed them whole in the United States, the family is now isolated in an even more ominous and resentful environment at home. The world they face becomes more hostile as they attempt to rebuild their lives, making the adjustment even more difficult.

By removing his characters from their familiar social circles and setting them free from any ties to their heritage, Lynch heightens the sense of alienation.

Europe is more rumor than truth, and the unyielding power of nature rules over man and woman in the remote townland of Carnarvon, which is situated on the world's periphery and isolated from larger social networks.

In the harsh winter of his mind, wolves roamed openly in the frozen tracks. Barnabas notices a corruption developing in himself and everything around him.

There is friction between the returning emigrant and nature, the locals, and even the past.

Famine huts open to the sky have lost all significance to him, and he finds it hard to fathom the life of the bare feet who formerly inhabited this land.

Even though he's very similar to his fellow citizens, he's still considered a local stranger and is therefore expected to be different just because he's been abroad.

From laid out in cold white sheets to a blood horizon or even a yellow morning—a scene in which the sun's warmth coaxes vegetation to emerge from the ground—the sky is a powerful metaphor. He watched a devil-wind lash up a vortex union of grass and depart, an instant of pure circumferential force that rushed it into a furious being, a whirling circle.

The descriptive style's depth drives the situation forward with violent and graphic visuals.

The story gains a sense of urgency in its depiction of the outsider's violent interactions with the community, but it also manages to convey human tenderness and meticulous attention to domestic detail, such the invitation to smell the smoke-damaged sheets, as if they had taken an imprint of the day, a stripe of dark on one of them beside a stripe of near white.

When it comes to storytelling, Lynch is gifted.

This becomes a previously unwritten version of Donegal as the novel's threads are tautened and drawn together into a confident finale.

Here we hear the full range of the Irish vernacular, yet it's as if the story's language had traversed the American prairies, passed through countless time zones, and then settled back into its original soil.

Grace 2017:

Love, grief, and the power of forgiveness are important ideas throughout the book.

In defiance of a speeding automobile, a young man, who is still a teenager, stands on a wide road.

Set in western Ireland in 1845, this is the first year of the Irish Potato Famine, also known as the Great Hunger. Six horses pull a carriage as they race along, the coachman lashing them to speed up the ride.

During the four years of the famine, about one million people perished as a result of starvation and diseases caused by it. Another one million is left.

After two-fifths of the population's food supply—depending on potato crops that failed—was threatened, many fled to the highways in search of relief.

Prefiguring our cultural dread of a zombie apocalypse are the itinerant beggars, wanderers, and wandering corpses. This is the tale of Grace, a people who fought for every moment of their lives, never satisfied with anything less than the best.

Grace Coyle's mother chops off her hair and forces her to leave their Donegal cottage when she is fourteen years old. You're the one who's strong now, her mom says. Try to get a job. Return in twelve months.

As Grace embarks on her journey to survive, her younger brother, Colly, follows suit. Colly is a practical and resourceful presence who helps Grace. Standing in the center of the road is a young man named Bart, who is also an ally. Bart stands out as the story's most interesting protagonist to me.

As far as two young people fighting for their lives can feel love, Grace and Bart do. She knows they are ancient and young and will never die. at least once in a while.

However, romance does not apply here. The most resolute characters in this book ultimately succumb to fate and the passage of time, despite their assurances that death will never strike them.

The moral of the narrative is that believing you are an exception is essential for survival, but that idea isn't enough to get you through the terrible winters and hunger.

Grace is putting herself in the shoes of a survivor, a strong person. But she is not one of the fortunate when snow covers the ground and food is scarce.

Grace struggles with the identity she must adopt to endure, as well as the boundaries of her change. She had previously questioned, Is it possible for a fish to transform into a bird? Perhaps it's quite possible.

There are a lot of changes that Grace goes through, and she doesn't choose any of them.

She begins as a girl on a mountain and undergoes a lot of changes, including becoming a boy named Tim, a cattle drover; a developing woman betrayed by her period; a bandit; the pirate queen of Connaught; Deirdre of the Sorrows; Grainne, Diarmuid's love; a zombie; a corpse; a miraculous creation of God; the girl who refuses to speak up; the girl who is

Grace has had males repeatedly ask, What are you?

Mostly, the ghosts who accompany Grace on her trip are there to provide her with sustenance. Both the specters and the memory must depart in the final analysis.

He was nominated for the Walter Scott Prize and the Kerry Group Irish Novel of the Year in 2018 for his third novel, Grace.

Beyond the Sea 2019:

Lynch, who is usually likened to Cormac McCarthy, has managed to reel in a few fish since 2013.

Ideas of home and belonging are central to the narrative.

Experienced fisherman Bolivar, sometimes called Porky, has done something foolish. His big hands and tape-bound plastic sandals are telltale signs.

He wants to reel in enough fish to pay for repairs before his pursuers lop off his ears. Hector, his temporary assistant, is an awkward teenager who wears a pirate logo sweatshirt and has no experience fishing anywhere other than the local lagoon. He isn't winning him over.

An elderly man whose songs are sung to the bones of the dead is one of several indicators of their impending journey that Bolivar finds scattered throughout the South American beach where he stores his boat. Bolivar and Hector need to be making a beeline for port instead of venturing out into the impending storm.

Upon first glance, Beyond the Sea appears to be more of a film than a book. It's a black-and-white two-hander set in the mid-1950s, maybe, with a familiar existential setup: two men, stranded in the Pacific, need to understand each other for survival, but neither one is what he appears to be.

As the sun sets and the sky becomes darker, Bolivar and Hector cast their lines for two hours. Despite the excellent fishing, the storm is approaching and catches them off guard. The vessel bottoms out.

When the engine dies, the satellites and the radio go silent as well. From this point on, as their health worsens and rescue becomes an increasingly remote possibility, Lynch will keep us interested by having the two men converse about survival, life, death, and the meaning of being human and believing in a higher power.

To no one's surprise, Bolivar views the world as without answer; he believes that one can only interact with it physically rather than intellectually. It remains as it is, he says again. Thus, your agency is a manifestation of who you are, and you are what you are. Hector, on the other hand, appears malleable and anemic; he's attached to his phone and then grieves when it's lost.

The person he is right now—the one in the boat, as opposed to the one on land—is an illusion. He considers it a short-term solution put in place to address his current predicament.

It makes no difference how I slice it; I am not both here and there. I am neither nothing nor everything; I am neither. Bolivar, unimpressed, rubs the leg of the statue while trying to obtain an erection at night; he constructs an effigy of the Virgin Mary out of floating objects and prays for things to go back to how they were; he is desperately trying to find a place to stand.

As we turn the pages, we find that they're still alive, nevertheless drifting slowly westwards through the foul floating garbage dump of the Pacific Gyre. Lynch's poetic and deceptively supportive prose softens for us, but it never escapes the actual condition: indications of the final sickness, imaginary abuse, and dread of the journey, including a lightning flare so remote that it seems to belong to another age and a fleeting unintelligible sense of some other world caught in a shark's eyes.

You could not have predicted so many things would happen at once, Bolivar thinks, reflecting on the magnitude and rapidity of the calamity and how quickly one's perception of reality may shift from one extreme to the other.

In this book, men are defined as individuals whose understanding of their situations is constrained by hunger, material necessity, and an inclination to keep to themselves. It could have been one of those books about manhood.

Rather, it evolves into something more lyrical, yet icy, shocking, and self-aware.

Prophet Song is the most depressing of Lynch's four books that deal with Irish history and the hardships endured by Lynch's characters. The others are Red Sky in the Morning (2013), The Black Snow (2014), Grace (2017), and Beyond the Sea (2019).

I come from a tragic worldview, he admitted with a smile.

He began working on the novel's last line early on because it came to him first.

Chapter three

Prophet Song: A Literary Triumph at the 2023 Booker Prize

Paul Lynch's Prophet Song was the 2023 Booker Prize-winning novel.

On November 26, 2023, he was presented with the prize.

It is widely believed that the Booker Prize, which has been awarded annually since 1969 for novels written in English and published in the United Kingdom or Ireland, can have a profound impact on the careers of its winners.

Among those who have won before include Salman Rushdie, Hilary Mantel, Margaret Atwood, and Ian McEwan.

Having herself been nominated for the £50,000 ($63,000) prize twice, this year's judges chair, Esi Edugyan, stated:

Listening to Prophet Song, which follows a terrified woman as she tries to save her family in a totalitarian Ireland, shakes us out of our cynicism. From the very beginning, we were uneasy, engulfed, and plagued by the pervasive claustrophobia of Lynch's masterfully crafted universe.

Prophet Song vividly portrays contemporary social and political concerns. Truthful and devastating, readers will not soon forget the cautions it contains.

Robert Webb, Adjoa Andoh, poet Mary Jean Chan, and professor James Shapiro were among the assessors who, according to Edugyan, lauded Lynch's linguistic choices.

Here Lynch achieves linguistic accomplishments that are breathtaking to behold by stretching the sentence to its limit. As a poet at heart, he knows how to make reading an emotional experience through the use of repetition and repeated themes. Bold and courageous, this is an emotional storytelling accomplishment.

Lynch was declared the winner after a six-hour deliberation on Saturday, November 25, 2023, according to Edugyan. It is important to note that the decision-making process did not result in a unanimous decision.

As for whether or not the far-right-inspired incident in Dublin last Thursday was discussed, she stated that it had been brought up but wasn't a major consideration.

This award recognizes the best work in literature. Does this book achieve artistic success? That is the guiding idea. Global events cannot determine the outcome of the book contest. Still, we aimed for a title that conveyed the essence of the problem we're currently facing. There was something universal and relevant in all six books.

Edugyan made it clear that discussions about reviews were not included in their statement. You should remain unmoved by anything. We were on the hunt for a writer who was challenging conventions and making strides in form, narrative, and language.

Lynch has written five novels: Beyond the Sea, Grace (which was named Irish Novel of the Year by the Kerry Group in 2018), The

Black Snow, Red Sky in the Morning, and Prophet Song.

Oneworld, an independent publishing house, released Prophet Song. They were the winners of the prize in 2015 and 2016, respectively, for books by Marlon James (A Brief History of Seven Killings) and Paul Beatty (The Sellout).

The publisher and editor, Juliet Mabey, continues to publish authors that play on the margins, regardless of whether they produce monetarily or not, according to Lynch. Because many of the major publishing houses' imprints are risk-averse, intriguing indie houses like Oneworld and Fitzcarraldo keep winning awards.

Love, loss, faith, and uncertainty are some of the themes explored in the book.

Lynch devoted months to penning the wrong book before turning her attention to Prophet Song. On a Friday afternoon, he realized that it had died.

Opening a new Word document, the first page of Prophet Song practically appeared to him as it appears in the novel the following Monday as he sat in his shed at the foot of his yard in Dublin.

It was one of the miracles in his literary career, he said. I had no idea what I was going to write, but those first few lines encoded the entire meaning of the book.

On the first page, we see a knock on a door in a Dublin suburb.

Eilish Stack's husband, Larry, is a union leader in the teaching profession, and two agents from the newly established Irish secret police are on the hunt for him.

The disappearance of Eilish's husband and oldest kid pulls us into her life from the start of the book to its tragic conclusion.

Civil war erupts from dwindling freedoms, curfews, censorship, and surveillance. To paraphrase Hemingway, democracies fall slowly and then all at once.

Lynch dubbed the book an experiment in radical empathy, and the depictions of a city bombarded with artillery and walls covered with pictures of loved ones gone missing make one think of the current war zones across the globe.

The emergence of the far right and the plight of refugees are further concerns. A week before his book's victory, anti-immigration rioting rocked Dublin. The timing of this should serve as a wake-up call, Lynch echoed. This is the far right. It's not big, but it's here.

Since its inception in 1969, the most prestigious English-language fiction prize has gone to six Irish authors; he is the first since 2018's Anna Burns for Milkman to do so.

He was given the all-clear after undergoing cancer treatment, and this accolade comes a little over a year after his diagnosis.

In Prophet Song, we see the refugee crisis and the growth of political fanaticism.

The protagonist of the book, Eilish Stack, is determined to do everything it takes to protect her family as she struggles to make sense of a horrific social breakdown while her husband, the union leader, is jailed by the secret police.

Lynch made the following remarks after being honored:

Writing this book was not a picnic. The logical side of me thought that authoring this novel would ruin my career. Regardless, I was still obligated to write the book. This is an area where we are utterly powerless.

In addition, he expressed gratitude to all the kids of this world who need our safety, yet have lived, and continue to live because of the terrors portrayed throughout this book.

I am incredibly grateful, Lynch chimed in. I am bringing the Booker home to Ireland with immense pleasure.

The next day, during a news conference following his award presentation, Lynch expressed his astonishment at the violent disruptions that had occurred on Dublin streets the week before.

We may see what's happening in Dublin in the novel as a warning; I know that energy is always bubbling beneath the surface.

Lynch claimed he was distinctly not a political novelist and that the theme of grief throughout his work, which follows a wife whose husband is abducted by the young Irish secret police.

Lynch responded to the question of whether or not real-life events served as inspiration for his book's dystopian Ireland setting by saying:

I was attempting to perceive contemporary anarchy. the discontent in democracies in the West. The Syrian issue is the complete collapse of a nation, the magnitude of its refugee crisis, and the Western world's complete lack of concern. One of the goals of the Prophet Song is to demonstrate extreme empathy. We need to face the issue head-on if we want to get a better grasp on it.

Therefore, I aimed to add realism to the dystopian to make it more profound. My goal in writing this book was to make the reader experience the situation first hand rather than merely inform them about it.

Lynch's victory caps off a remarkable year for Irish literature.

Paul Murray's The Bee Sting was shortlisted for two prizes, and Elaine Feeney and Sebastian Barry were named to the shortlist.

Last week, the book was named Irish Novel of the Year at the Irish Book Awards.

Without the backing of the Irish state, none of this would have been possible, he stated.

This book received two Arts Council bursaries throughout its four-year publication. Great literary figures like Beckett and Joyce don't merely create masterpieces; they also inject our culture with an immense amount of energy, and we continue to draw from it, consciously or not.

Paul Lynch, an Irish novelist, claimed that the global trickster had been manipulating his life in a mad fashion.

I began writing the novel in 2018, and since then, a lot has happened: my son was born; he suffered from long-term COVID-19, which made writing difficult sometimes; he battled cancer and went through a divorce.

And just like that, I won the most prestigious award for modern literature. When asked about winning, he responds, There's a broad sensation of unreality.

I've entered the alternate reality of my own Sliding Doors story.

The creative process isn't logical. You can't just ignore this; I'm going to deal with it.

Taking one's children on a small boat with strangers in the middle of the night—that is what he aimed to convey to the reader—in a state of frantic desperation. He explained that it was important to maintain eye contact. hooking the reader with an authentic feeling of being inevitable, so they can't help but keep reading. I refuse to look at this, they can't claim.

The author uses lengthy, poetically laden sentences devoid of paragraph breaks and speech marks to bring the 300-page nightmare to life. A lack of space for air was his complaint.

You're stuck. There shouldn't be any white space, and the events are drawing you in; therefore, the paragraphs aren't there. Just as Eilish is suffocating, the reader should feel the same way.

Chapter four

Lynch, an Icon of Irish Literature on a Global Scale: His Legacy and Influence

Paul Lynch is now widely recognized as one of Ireland's most compelling literary figures because of his innate talent for narrative and theatrical flair.

His works have won numerous awards and solidified his reputation as a master storyteller due to their lyricism, deep understanding of human nature, and boldness in tackling difficult topics.

Lynch's first novel, Red Sky in the Morning, was a moving story that showcased his talent for storytelling and the depth of his characters' minds.

Beyond the Sea and Grace, two of his later novels, further cemented his status as a literary giant; both books enthralled readers with their complex plots, examination of timeless subjects, and memorable protagonists and antagonists.

Lynch achieved new heights in 2023 as a writer with the publication of Prophet Song, which garnered him the esteemed Booker Prize.

His literary influence grew exponentially after this prestigious award propelled him to international prominence.

Lynch has creative ambitions that go well beyond his home county of Donegal, while the harsh landscapes of his hometown are common settings for his novels.

His artistic leanings suggest an interest in delving into the many facets of the human condition by taking him to the varied landscapes and lively cultures of Russia, Central America, and the American frontier.

Lynch's prose is famously stylized, and his vivid imagery and expressive language are hallmarks of his literary style, which draws inspiration from the works of several unknown Latin American literary giants as well as Cormac McCarthy, William Faulkner, and Herman Melville.

He has a dedicated fan base and high praise from critics for his skill in crafting complex stories that expertly combine historical details with modern issues.

Lynch is still a very driven and ambitious writer, even after all his literary success; he is always looking for new ways to push his creativity and explore different genres.

His exploration of historical drama, pastoral gothic, and the picaresque reveals his versatility and unfaltering commitment to storytelling, as he is eager to experiment and push the boundaries.

Lynch's second book, The Black Snow, provides evidence of his storytelling prowess. Barnabas Kane, the protagonist, is evocative of tragic protagonists from Shakespeare's plays, and the story explores the depths of human sorrow and resilience against the backdrop of 1945 in Donegal.

Lynch demonstrates his mastery of language and capacity to immerse readers in his story in the novel's opening scene, which is a detailed account of a farmhouse fire.

Lynch deftly crafts a world in Grace, maybe her most approachable work, where high concept meets raw emotion and language meets character. An edgy outlaw with the heart of True Grit's Mattie Ross sets off on a quest that tests her worldview and her understanding of human connection.

Among Lynch's most celebrated works, the novel stands out for its historical sweep and compelling narrative.

Last but not least, Paul Lynch is an outstanding and inspiring writer. His profound insights into humanity, impeccable narrative skills, and steadfast commitment to his art have enchanted people all over the globe.

His works, which are filled with lyricism, complex stories, and memorable characters, have placed him among the most esteemed Irish novelists of our era.

He left an everlasting impression on literature with his works, which have inspired and enriched readers for decades.

Chapter five

Praise, Honour, and International Notoriety Earned

The following are just a few of the many accolades and nominations that Paul Lynch has received:

Irish Francophonie Ambassadors' Literary Award: 2020 Recipient Announced

In 2019, I was shortlisted for the Prix Jean Monnet for European Literature.

2019: 2019 Prix Littérature Monde: Finalists Announced

2019: Nominated for the Grand Prix de L'Héroïne

Award for Best Irish Novel 2018: Kerry Group

In 2018, I was on the shortlist for the Walter Scott Prize in Historical Fiction.

Selected for the 2018 William Saroyan Prize in International Writing

2016: Best Foreign Novel Award Winner: Prix Libr'à Nous

Laureate of the 2016 Prix des Lecteurs Privat

Ireland Francophonie Ambassadors' Literary Award: Selected for the 2016 Finalists

Prix Femina: 2015: Listed

2015: Longlisted for the Prix du Roman Fnac

2014: Listed in the running for the Prix du Meilleur Livre Étranger, named the world's best foreign book,

Shortlisted for the 2014 Prix du Premier Roman (First Novel Prize)

2012: Bord Gais Irish Book of the Year: Honored with a Bronze Medal

Marianne Gunn O'Brien of the Marianne Gunn O'Brien Literary Agency represents Paul Lynch.

He contributed frequently to The Sunday Times' cinema section and served as lead film critic for the Sunday Tribune in Ireland from 2007 to 2011.

Chapter six

Challenges in Life and Work: Finding a Happy Medium Between Achieving Your Goals and Facing Difficulties

Paul Lynch, a renowned figure in literature, also endured incessant hardships and trials. What sets him apart, though, is his incredible resilience in the face of adversity.

Paul wished to demonstrate that the concept of the world's apocalypse appears often in history. The belief that the world will abruptly end at some point in your lifetime—this is the Armageddon concept—is fiction. However, the end of the world occurs repeatedly. He warned that it shows up in your town and starts pounding on your door.

Lynch had a knock on the door shortly after delivering the Prophet Song manuscript.

He was 45 years old, thought he was writing brilliantly, and suddenly a kidney tumor was discovered.

That thing you carry around with you all your life, that invincibility shield, just shatters into a million pieces when you sit in that chair and hear you have cancer, he added. To your former self, it's nearly unfathomable how vulnerable you become.

It was indefensible that he would be absent from the lives of his two children.

The chances of it coming back after immunotherapy and an operation when he donated a kidney to the hospital incinerator are extremely low, according to his physicians. I believe them when they say that. I'm just going to go ahead and do it.

A year after his surgery, he found out he had been shortlisted for the Booker Prize on the very same day.

During this period, he divorced his wife. Because of all the upheaval in my life, I'm only now beginning to piece together my identity. Every aspect of my day-to-day self is being reconstructed.

Chapter six

Less Well-Known Elements of Paul Lynch's Life: A Window into His Private Life

Away from the limelight, renowned Irish writer Paul Lynch has a peaceful family life in Dublin with his wife and two children, known for his enthralling stories.

Paul Lynch deliberately keeps his personal life out of the spotlight, despite his literary fame. His spouse, whose identity is kept secret, intentionally steers clear of public appearances and shares her husband's inclination for seclusion.

Like her fictional counterpart, who fearlessly avoids the limelight despite his fame, she is steadfast in her desire for privacy.

Her steadfast support, as the unsung hero behind the scenes, is the foundation upon which Paul Lynch's remarkable literary accomplishments rest.

They have been together for nearly 20 years, and they are now the doting parents of two wonderful children.

Paul Lynch has been tight-lipped about his love life since he met his present wife.

Paul Lynch is a model of a committed husband and father who manages a busy writing career while still enjoying a rich personal life filled with deep relationships with his extended family.

Even though he is quite secretive about some things, he generously lets his fans and admirers in on little bits of his life off the record.

Though he now calls Dublin home, Paul Lynch is busy tending to his beloved family life and penning enthralling stories.

Chapter seven

Net worth

The celebrated Irish novelist Paul Lynch has accumulated an impressive fortune of almost $5 million.

His enormous fortune is a reflection of the fruitful and extensive career he had as a literary genius.

His enthralling stories, deep understanding of humanity, and skill as a storyteller have made him a household name in Ireland and around the world.

The world was introduced to Lynch's distinctive combination of lyricism, psychological depth, and evocative narrative with his debut novel, Red Sky in Morning, which launched his road to literary fame and financial success.

Lynch's captivating story enthralled both critics and readers, propelling her to literary stardom.

In the years that followed, novels like Beyond the Sea and Grace added to Lynch's already stellar reputation.

He has a loyal fan base and high praise from critics for his mastery of story structure, ability to delve into timeless subjects, and creation of memorable characters.

His literary impact has increased as a result of readers all over the world enjoying his works in other languages.

Lynch has achieved great literary success, which has brought him both critical acclaim and financial windfalls.

With over a million copies sold, his novels have brought him a substantial amount of money from royalties and book sales. Lynch's Grace won the esteemed Kerry Group Irish Novel of the Year award, among many others, for Lynch's literary achievements.

In 2023, Lynch won the prestigious Booker Prize for his novel Prophet Song, which elevated his literary career to new heights.

In addition to increasing his wealth, this prestigious award solidified Lynch's position as a literary luminary.

Lynch's influence goes well beyond the money he has made.

Innumerable people have found comfort, inspiration, and insight into the human condition in his books.

Many have been moved to tears, had their worldviews shaken, and developed a love of storytelling as a result of his writings.

Paul Lynch's immense wealth is a testament to his exceptional skill, steadfast commitment to his work, and significant influence on the literary landscape.

His works as a gifted storyteller will live on in the hearts and minds of readers everywhere, and his novels will have a lasting impact on many more.

Conclusion

We are in wonder of Paul Lynch's lasting legacy, proof of the transformational power of storytelling, as we wrap up our examination of his remarkable literary journey.

He is rightfully considered one of the greatest writers of all time for his impeccable grasp of the English language, deep understanding of the human experience, and steadfast commitment to his work.

Lynch's books have an international audience because they speak to people of many backgrounds and cultures.

The characters he created with such care and genuineness have become friends, confidantes, and reflections of ourselves.

Their adventures force us to face our innermost feelings, delve into the intricacies of human connections, and face the commonalities that unite us all.

Lynch has had an impression on the narrative that goes far beyond the written word.

His words have brought to mind the profound impact that stories can have on our lives, how they can open our minds to new ideas, and how they can ignite our imaginations.

His books have done more than just keep readers occupied; they have also ignited ideas, discussions, and debates that continue long after they have finished reading.

May Paul Lynch's profound impact on literature never fade, and may his words always reverberate within us, leading us through life's twists and turns.

We hope that his stories will guide us and remind us of the strength of the human spirit and that they will shine a light on our pathways.

Rip.

Printed in Great Britain
by Amazon

33508863R00051